THE GREATEST TREASURE

Philip Saumarez and the voyage of the *Centurion*

Guernsey Museum

Published by Guernsey Museums & Galleries

© 1994 States of Guernsey

Edited by Sally Rousham

ISBN 1 871560 86 1

Illustrations from the 1748 edition of *Anson's Voyage Round
the World in the Years 1740-4:* engravings after drawings by
Lieutenant Peircy Brett.

THE DE SAUSMAREZ FAMILY

GENERATIONS of the de Sausmarez family of Guernsey distinguished themselves in the Royal Navy. The first to enter the service was Philip Saumarez who, in 1740-44, accompanied Anson on his famous expedition to the South Seas and around the world.

The voyage was an epic of human endurance and suffering culminating in the capture of the Spanish treasure ship, *Nuestra Señora de Cobadonga.*

The story is told here largely in the words of Lieutenant Philip Saumarez; they are taken from his log and a long letter he wrote to his family in Guernsey.

Philip was the third son of Matthew de Sausmarez and Anne Durrell. He was born in Guernsey on 17th November 1710. He was educated to the age of 11 at the grammar school in Jersey and then in Southampton - where he was sent to learn mathematics, classics, and English. He was introduced to the Royal Navy by his uncle, Captain James Durrell, and in February 1726 he joined the *Weymouth,* then attached to the Baltic station. He served in the Mediterranean and the West Indies and was promoted to lieutenant in 1737. After a visit to Guernsey and Jersey to see friends and family, in December 1739, he joined the *Centurion* under Commodore Anson as Second Lieutenant.

Philip's younger brother, Thomas, also served on the *Centurion* during the circumnavigation.

The best-known naval member of the family was Admiral Lord James Saumarez (1757-1836), Philip's posthumous nephew, who distinguished himself in the War of American Independence and the French Wars.

Note: two branches of the family spell their names slightly differently. The sea-going men, Philip, Thomas, and James, dropped the 'de' and the second 's' from the name supposedly to sound less French.

To Annoy and Distress Spain

Spain under Philip V was still a great power with a vast empire in the Americas. In Britain George II was on the throne with Robert Walpole as prime minister.

Peru and Mexico had fabulous silver and gold mines which the British eyed with envy. When war broke out with Spain in 1739 (the famous War of Jenkins Ear) the British government decided to attack Spain through her colonies.

A fleet under Admiral Vernon was despatched to the Caribbean and a secondary expedition, under Commodore George Anson, was sent round Cape Horn to the Pacific to 'annoy and distress' the Spanish.

THE ROYAL NAVY

IN the 18th century the Royal Navy was by far the biggest, most complex, and most expensive department of state. Together with the Royal dockyards it was the largest industrial organisation in Europe.

The Ships

Men-of-war were divided into six 'rates'. The *Centurion*, with 60 guns, was classified as a 4th rate. She was built at Portsmouth and launched in 1732 and was finally broken up at Chatham in 1769.

The men-of-war which made up Anson's squadron were:-

Centurion: 4th rate, 60 guns, 1005 tons, 400 complement

Gloucester: 4th rate, 50 guns, 866 tons, 300 complement

Severn: 4th rate, 48 guns, 683 tons, 300 complement

Pearle: 5th rate, 42 guns, 559 tons, 250 complement

Wager: 6th rate, 24 guns, 559 tons, 160 complement

Tryall: sloop, 14 guns, 201 tons, 100 complement.

For the first part of the voyage they were accompanied by two merchant victuallers, known as pinks, the *Anna* and the *Industry*.

The Officers

Philip Saumarez's route into the Royal Navy was typical of his time, although at 16 he was older than most new recruits. He joined his first ship in 1726.

Officers were usually recruited from the younger sons of the gentry. The alternative careers open to them were the church and the army. One required a university education, which could be costly, and the other required capital to purchase a commission (and, in a fashionable regiment, a private income as well). By contrast, the Royal Navy provided a young gentleman with free professional training.

Despite the hardships, a life at sea offered the romance of travel and adventure and the lure of prize money, but it was said that officers had to be taken on as boys otherwise they would not be

A view of the land of PATAGONIA a little to the northward of PORT S.t IULIAN.

able to endure the discomfort of life at sea. They all began their careers as ratings and had to learn seamanship - going aloft and how to reef, steer, and navigate.

In the more senior ranks political connections were useful, but promotion to lieutenant and captain was dictated by experience and ability.

The Commodore, George Anson, was born in 1697 at Shugborough in Staffordshire. He entered the Navy in 1712 and was made a captain in 1724. The *Centurion* expedition left Anson a wealthy man. He was made a Rear Admiral of the Blue in 1744, and, after a victorious battle with the French off Cape Finisterre in 1747, he was made Baron Anson of Soberton. In 1751 he became First Lord of the Admiralty.

Anson was a reserved man who did not care much for society. He was more popular in the Navy than in the political world; however, he married the daughter of the Lord Chancellor. His attention to standards of training and conduct bore fruit in the naval victories of the Seven Years War (1756-63); his administrative

reforms earned him the nickname 'Father of the Royal Navy'. He died in June 1762.

Several of the other officers who served under Commodore Anson on the *Centurion* went on to become admirals. They included Peircy Brett, who made the drawings that were later engraved to illustrate the published account of the circumnavigation. He started the voyage as First Lieutenant on the *Gloucester*, and by the end was captain of the *Centurion* under Anson. He went on to become an Admiral of the Blue and a Lord Commissioner of the Admiralty.

Augustus Keppel, second son of the Earl of Albermarle, went to sea at the age of ten. He joined the *Centurion* as a midshipman and returned as a second lieutenant - aged 19. He became a Rear Admiral during the Seven Years War and First Lord of the Admiralty in 1782.

Hyde Parker went to sea in a merchant ship before joining the Royal Navy in 1738. He became a captain in 1748 and in 1762 had the good fortune to capture another Manila galleon, the *Santissima Trinidad* with £600,000 of treasure on board. He eventually reached the rank of Vice Admiral, but was murdered after his ship was wrecked in the Malabar Islands in 1782.

Charles Saunders was a 'brave and excellent officer' who left England as Second Lieutenant of the *Centurion*. He was given command of the *Tryall* until she had to be scuttled after which he returned home from Macao. In 1747 he was with Lord Hawke's squadron in the action in which Philip Saumarez was killed. He later became an Admiral of the Blue and First Lord of the Admiralty.

Philip Saumarez's younger brother, Thomas, was also on Anson's circumnavigation; he is not referred to in Philip's log though he is mentioned in private correspondence. He served as a midshipman at first on the *Centurion* and then, under his brother's command, on the captured Manila galleon. In 1758, as a post-captain, Thomas was in command of the *Antelope,* of 50 guns, when she captured the 64-gun French man-of-war *Belliquex.* When this ship was taken into the Royal Navy, Thomas was given command, but he had to be invalided home from the West Indies and died in 1766.

In addition to the commissioned officers there were warrant officers; these were specialist craftsmen such as sailmakers and carpenters and were responsible directly to the captain. The master of a Royal Naval ship was the warrant officer in charge of navigation.

The Crew

The age of the crew varied from boys of ten to old men of fifty, but the majority of crew were young bachelors.

Some of the men were pressed, but others joined a ship from choice. Life at sea was arduous and often dangerous, but at a time when most ordinary people lived in poverty, employment at sea often paid better than any work available on the land, and for many the prospect of regular meals was a real attraction. On 23rd March 1740, while moored at Spithead, Saumarez wrote in his log: *... I returned with the tender having brought 39 volunteers from Jersey* and on 24th April he wrote: *our tender with the second lieutenant and 32 men went out to impress seamen in the Channel.*

The crew, officers and men, did not enrol in the service as such but joined a particular ship under its commander. The notoriously savage discipline and sharp class distinctions of the Royal Navy in the last years of the 18th century did not apply in the 1740s.

A regiment of marines for boarding and raiding parties was taken with the squadron which added to the overcrowding on the ships. Many of these men were more or less decrepit pensioners from the Chelsea Hospital and most of them died before they reached Cape Horn. Of the 552 marines who set sail none survived the voyage.

LIFE AT SEA

THE 'wooden world' of His Majesty's ships was unlike life ashore: sailors' dress, manners and language were quite strange to the outsider.

A ship's day ran from noon to noon - when the officers took sights and plotted the ship's position. Half the junior officers and crew, other than specialist tradesmen, were on watch at any time. Each watch lasted for four hours except for the two two-hour dog watches between 4 and 8 p.m. There were no clocks on board, time was measured in watches. A half-hour sandglass was kept running and a bell was rung each time it was turned, at eight bells the watch was changed. Men on the watches never got more than four hours sleep at a time; and all hands were called ('piped') out when needed to handle the ship.

The men slept in hammocks slung close together on the gun deck. During the day hammocks were rolled and stored along the sides of the quarter deck and forecastle where they provided protection from flying splinters when the ship went into action.

Commissioned officers had tiny cabins to themselves; the captain had a spacious cabin at the after end of the ship.

'Stench and nastyness ...'

Most of the time the gun ports, which were only a few feet above the waterline, had to be kept closed. Any light and air came down the hatch. Although the atmosphere below decks could become appalling, men who had been aloft tending the sails often felt that the last thing they wanted was more fresh air.

Life at sea was governed by the weather. While in command of the sloop Tryall, battling on the approach to Cape Horn, Saumarez wrote in his log:-

10th March, 1741:
The first part moderate with small rain, the middle and later fresh gales with hard squalls, with much snow and a large hollow sea at a.m. Got in the spritsail yard fore and aft to ease the sloop who laboured extremely, and reefed

the foresail. At noon had lost sight of the Commodore and squadron, the air being so extremely thick with large quantities of snow which fell; at the same time had it exceeding cold. Our masts and yards were all crusted over with frozen snow.

At other times the ships were becalmed in merciless heat. When they were heavily loaded, with stores or booty, they were low in the water and the ports could not be opened. With half the crew sick, many with dysentery, the stench below decks was appalling.

23rd April 1741:-

... some intervals of calms and sunshine which we used in repairing and setting up our rigging which was broken and shattered and took the tarpaulins off our gratings and hatchways to air between decks and clean the ship as much as lay in our power; and really it is scarce conceivable what a stench and nastyness our poor sick people had caused among each other and which contributed to infect those who struggle against distemper.

Food

Meals were cooked in the galley on the upper deck under the forecastle where there was a brick structure fuelled by wood or charcoal. There were ovens for baking and large coppers in which all the meat was boiled.

The crew ate in 'messes' of six men on the gundeck; the officers ate in the wardroom.

The standard weekly ration included meat (beef or pork), pease, oatmeal, butter, cheese, and bread. Meat was salted and fish dried - there was no other means of preserving food. Live animals - sheep, cattle, goats, and fowl - were carried on board to provide a supply of fresh food for the officers.

A ship could stay at sea only as long as its water lasted. Alcohol was added to water to make it drinkable. The officers drank wine and spirits, the men beer or, when that ran out, diluted rum.

Scurvy

The scourge of life at sea was scurvy. It was the cause of many more deaths than enemy action, falls from the rigging, or shipwreck combined. We now know that it is caused by a lack of vitamin C, but vitamins were not discovered until the 20th century.

Saumarez and his sea-going contemporaries realised that there was some link between diet and scurvy, but did not understand the true cause of the disease or how to cure it. Officers suffered less than the men, probably due to their better diet and less crowded living conditions.

The first signs of scurvy would usually appear after four or five weeks at sea. If he received no vitamin C a victim would die after about a month.

There were two major outbreaks of scurvy during the voyage: between St Julians in Patagonia and Juan Fernandez and on the passage from Acapulco to the island of Tinian. A third of the crew died in the first, half of those remaining died in the second outbreak.

The *Gloucester* set sail with 396 men on board. Scurvy was so bad that by the time she had to be scuttled only 97 were left alive - not enough men to sail the ship - and most of them were sick.

The connection between citrus fruits, onions, and other vegetables and scurvy, was made by James Lind, a naval surgeon, writing in 1748-54. He based some of his conclusions on information gained from the experience of this circumnavigation.

Distemper is the consequence of long voyages ...

The association of dirt with disease was not properly understood. However, it was believed that infection was spread by foul air so whenever possible the ships were 'sweetened' by scrubbing with oil and vinegar which also cleaned them.

Saumarez wrote to his family:-
During this time, the scurvy made terrible havoc among us, especially the soldiers, who being either infirm old men or raw inexperienced youths, soon lost their spirits, grew sick and disabled, and from the stench they occasioned, contributed to infect our seamen.

This distemper is the consequence of long voyages, and exhibits itself in such dreadful symptoms as are scarcely credible, viz. asthma, pains in the limbs and joints, blotches all over the body, ulcers, idiotism, lunacy, convulsions, and sudden death. Nor can the physicians, with all their materia medica, *find a remedy for it equal to the smell of turf, grass, or a dish of greens.*

29th May 1741. Island of Chiloe 189 leagues:

... Had all our faculties awake to look out for the island, our people being grown to the last degree infirm and sick and few of them able to do their duty, falling down hourly ...

NAVIGATION

NAVIGATION was as much an art as a science in the mid-18th century.

The ship's master was in charge of navigation. Responsible directly to the captain, in status and pay this warrant officer was equal to the lieutenants. Saumarez and the other lieutenants also learnt navigation skills.

Latitude is a measure of a ship's north/south position; longitude is a measure of its east/west position. If the sky was clear to take sightings of the sun or stars, with a quadrant it was possible to plot a ship's latitude to within a few miles.

To calculate longitude it was necessary to know the exact time of day to establish the distance east or west of the Greenwich meridian at noon. An accurate ship's chronometer (which measured time) was not developed until the 1750s; in Saumarez's day, once out of sight of land, longitude was estimated by guesswork.

Thus it was that Anson's expedition set sail round the world without the ability to calculate its east/west position.

Charts

The charts (as sea maps are called) which Saumarez and his colleagues had to work with were many years old and hopelessly inadequate (this was before the extent of Australia, New Zealand, or the Antarctic was known to Europeans). Saumarez and the other lieutenants, Peircy Brett in particular, made amendments and more reliable charts as they sailed up the coast of South America.

13th April 1741. Cape Good Success 214 leagues:

… The currents having thus far deceived us with our frequent laying to and shortening sail. Squally. At 1 a.m. providentially clearing up discerned land right ahead about 2 leagues making like an island with 2 homocks and by my observation was probably an island

A Scale of Miles.

1   2   3   4   5   6

Her Way out

brought up with 2 Anchors

her Drift

The Arm. Pink

This ISLAND is call'd INCHIN by the Indians

PLAN
of a BAY and HARBOUR
on the Coast of CHILI:
Discovered by a Victualler
to COMMODORE ANSON'S Squadron
in the SOUTH SEA,
1741.

called Cape Noir laying off the Straits of Magellan. This was a most unexpected sight, esteeming ourselves at that time near 200 leagues off… we were in hopes at last to have weathered the Straits of Magellan.

4th May 1743. The Grand Ladrone distance 132 leagues 2 miles:

… At 8 p.m. tacked being in some doubt about the Bashee Islands which few of the charts mention and which are imperfectly set down by voyagers; Dampier lays them down in the latt. of 20°20'N but his observation of the south part of Formosa where we likewise observed differing from ours considerably, makes us suspect his account of the situation.

DEPARTURE: CROSSING THE ATLANTIC

25th December 1739, Portsmouth Harbour:

His Majesty's ship the Centurion lately come out of dock, her bottom sheathed and graved laying at her mooring abreast the dock, Portsmouth Harbour. Received my commission from the Commissioner's Office in this port as 3rd Lieutenant of His Majesty's Ship the Centurion. Captain George Anson Commander. Repaired immediately aboard and found her fitting out with great expedition for foreign service. Received on board 200 bags of bread containing 22,400 pounds, much broken by the driving of the tide. Blew exceedingly hard with severe cold weather. Received 21 pecks of beef [Saumarez goes on to list oil, water, pork, flour, butter, and vinegar] … Built up 4 cabins by order of the Navy Board for the marine officers intended on board.

The following months were spent taking supplies on board, fitting out the ship, and finding a crew and a regiment of marines.

'The signal to weigh …'

18th September 1740. Sailed from St Helens and anchored:

At 7 a.m. made the signal to weigh and made sail with His Majesty's ships the Gloucester, Severn, Pearle, Wager and Tryall sloop, with 2 merchant ships laden with provisions for our squadron.

The squadron was to act as escort to convoys as far as the Bay of Biscay, which delayed progress to the speed of the slowest ship.

26th October 1740. Ram Head 390 leagues:

Sent the Severn and Tryall sloop ahead to discover the island of Madeira. Oughtry and Murry deceased.

After 41 days at sea the squadron was able to take on supplies in Madeira. Many of the men, particularly the soldiers, were sick. They stayed a month at Madeira before striking off to cross the Atlantic to South America.

Sickness, mostly scurvy and dysentery, soon spread among the men, particularly in the doldrums. They were becalmed near the equator and additional ports were cut to allow more air into the overcrowded ship.

24th November 1740. Island of Madeira 587 leagues:
This day was more settled than the others but with frequent intervals of squalls and showers. Several of our men through the moisture and inconstancy of the air were attacked with fever and headaches. Not having had an observation through these last days found by this day's observation that I was 15 miles to the northward of my reckoning which confirms the general opinion of a northwest current setting near the equinoctial line.

25th November 1740. Island of Madeira 611 leagues:
Today had a serene cool air with a constant wind at south east. We now flatter ourselves to be got into a Trade Wind.

26th November 1740. Island of Madeira 635 leagues:
The whole part a constant moderate gale with fair weather. Richard Pearce an invalid deceased.

29th November 1740. Island of Madeira 746 leagues:
It blew a constant fresh gale. A severe clear sky. Pursuing our course to the south west. Amos Gordon and Edward Major, seamen, departed this life.

12th December 1740. Island of Madeira 1186 leagues:
… At 9 a.m. Mr Robert Weldon our purser being quite worn out departed this life. …

15th December 1740. Island of Madeira 1286 leagues:
Very uncertain squally weather with rain … David Redman a marine departed this life.

St Catherines

On 18th December the *Centurion* arrived at the island of St Catherines off the coast of Brazil. The island was held by the Portuguese, allies of England. While there repairs were made to the ships and fresh food and water were taken

A view of the north entrance of the harbour of St CATHERINES.

on board. The sick were moved to tents on shore; but 80 more men died, 28 of them from the crew of the Centurion.

21st December 1740. St Catherine's Harbour:

Half past noon we passed by the island the [Portuguese] governor resides on, saluted the fortification with 11 guns. ... The water both on the island and the Continent is excellent and preserved beyond what I ever observed. After having it on board some short time it discharged itself with a green putrid scum which subsided to the bottom and left the remainder as clear as crystal ...

The woods abound with several medicinal and aromatic plants. One might imagine oneself in a druggist's shop. As you traverse the woods the fruits are chiefly the orange, lemon, lime, citron, melons, grapes, guavas, with pineapple and many potatoes and onions. Here is great plenty of oxen with many pheasants, inferior to ours, but with abundance and monkeys and parrots all edible. They have a very singular bird called the toucan ...

In January the squadron set sail from St Catherines. The next rendezvous was the Port St Julian 1200 miles south on the desolate coast of Patagonia. The Pacific coast of South America was under Spanish, therefore hostile, influence.

We sailed hence on the 18th of January 1741, and soon after began to meet with uncertain, stormy weather, in which the Tryal sloop lost her mainmast, and was towed by one of the squadron; the rest separated from us, but as our rendezvous was at St Julien's, a port on the coast of Patagonia ... we rejoined them there, by which we heard of Pizarro's squadron, from whom we narrowly escaped off Pepy's Island. We stayed here eight days...

The coast here is a sulphurous and nitrous soil, abounding with salt lakes, but destitute of verdure, shrub, tree, or fresh water, and seems the seat of infernal spirits; nor indeed was there the trace of any animals, besides seals and birds. We here took in salt and refitted the sloop.

CAPE HORN: SAUMAREZ'S FIRST COMMAND

ON this leg of the voyage Captain Kidd, in command of the *Wager*, died. As a result Saumarez was put in temporary command of the sloop *Tryall* and in this capacity he led the squadron on the agonisingly long and dangerous journey round Cape Horn.

Captain Kidd's death made a revolution by promotion amongst us, and I was appointed first lieutenant of the Commodore; but my predecessor [Lieutenant Saunders], to whose command the sloop descended, was taken dangerously ill, and became incapable of taking possession of his charge. I was ordered to take command until his recovery; and here I must confess to you, I was sanguine enough to flatter myself with the same addition of good fortune, some favourable crisis in my behalf: but I was born to be unfortunate.

The *Severn* and the *Pearl* abandoned the attempt to round Cape Horn and turned for home. Saumarez assumed they had been wrecked. The rest of the squadron laboured on.

'Nothing but disasters ...'

We sailed hence on the 27th of February 1741: my station was a-head of the squadron, to keep sounding and make timely signals of danger. The 4th of March we discovered the entrance of the Strait of Magellan and on the 7th passed through the Strait le Main lying at the extremity of Terra del Fuego, between that and Staten Land.

This day was remarkably warm and favourable, and though in latitude 55°50' south, we began to look on the conquest of the Peruvian mines and principal towns in the Pacific sea as an amusement, which would naturally occur. From this time forward we met with nothing but disasters and accidents. Never were the passions of hope and fear so powerfully exercised; the very elements seemed combined against us. I commanded the sloop at the time of the

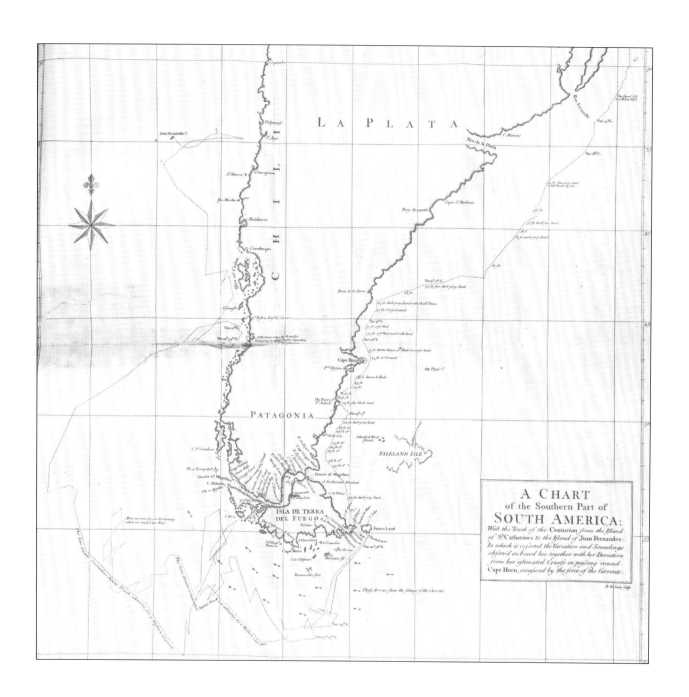

LA PLATA

CHILI

PATAGONIA

ISLA DE TERRA
DEL FUEGO

FALKLAND ISLE

A CHART
of the Southern Part of
SOUTH AMERICA;
With the Track of the Centurion from the Island
of St Catherines to the Island of Juan Fernandes;
In which is inserted the Variation and Soundings
observed on board her; together with her Deviation
from her estimated Course in passing round
Cape Horn, occasioned by the force of the Currents.

[20]

separations of the ships that returned home, being stationed to look out for islands of ice; and had to endure such fatigue from the severity of the weather, and the duty which the nature of the service necessarily brought on me, that really my life was hardly worth preserving at the expense of such hardships. Our own ships had several miraculous escapes, which, in the obscurity of the night and the violence of the weather, often endangered foundering the sloop.

22nd March 1741. Cape Good Success 176 leagues:
Stormy weather with violent squalls and hail. The weather very cold and uncomfortable, our people being continually wet and much harassed and jaded.

23rd March 1741. Cape Good Success 172 leagues:
Blew very hard with a large hollow sea breaking continually over us; our masts and rigging all coated with frozen snow and ice.

24th March 1741. Cape Good Success 177 leagues:
…The sloop hauled, being half-full of water with the seas which we had shipped and were obliged to keep bailing and pumping all night, our pumps being likewise but very indifferent, being continually choked up with sand.

25th March 1741. Cape Good Success 184 leagues:
Uncertain squally weather; the latter part blew exceptionally hard with much hail. Got our anchors in upon deck to ease our bows, the sloop labouring much and struck all our swivel guns off the decks. At 10 a.m. we were obliged to haul the foresail up and lay to not being able to carry sail any longer; being in danger of foundering and thereby lost sight of the squadron …

Having had the command of the sloop several weeks, I was at length superseded by her proper captain, who had recovered on board the Commodore's ship; and I returned to my post [as First Lieutenant on the Centurion] *…*

For the space of six weeks we seldom buried less than four or five daily, and at last it amounted to eight or ten; and I really believe that, had we stayed ten days longer at sea, we should have lost the ship for want of men to navigate her.

17th April 1741. Cape Good Success 228 leagues:
... George Ramsey seaman, Francis Sullivan and George Ruth soldiers departed this life.

18th April 1741. Cape Good Success 235 leagues:
... Allan Ellison and Ref Roberts, marines, deceased.

'The elements all confused'
There was a terrible storm towards the end of April. Then:-

27th April 1741. Cape Good Success 147 leagues:
Fair weather. Set up all our shrouds and back stays and fitted our rigging up against the next storm. Richard Dolby and Robert Hood seamen and William Thompson marine deceased. Set the topsails. Our men now began to decline a pace, the scurvy reigning among us and making terrible havoc.

12th May 1741. The Island of Succoro on Chile coast 55 leagues:
More gales. Weather very uncertain. At 4 p.m. handed the topsails. At 6 p.m. the wind shifting to the north west wore ship and stood to the eastward. John MacMannus, man-at-arms, deceased. Our ship's company was in most deplorable condition, the distemper gaining ground on our people daily.

17th May 1741. South of the Island of Chiloe, Island of Guaffo 12 leagues:
A continuation of stormy surprising weather, the elements seeming all confused. In the height of the squall had several violent claps of thunder; before the explosion of which a quick subtle fire ran along our decks which bursting made a report like a pistol and struck several of our men and officers who with the violence of the blow were black and blue in several places. This fire was attended with a strong sulphurous smell; at 4 p.m. our fore sheet broke which endangered splitting the sail ...

JUAN FERNANDEZ

THE *Centurion's* arrival at Juan Fernandez, an island off the coast of Chile, was delayed by the faulty judgement of the navigator, Justinian Nutt. However, in the meantime a Spanish squadron that had been waiting for Anson's ship to arrive had given up and left the island.

8th June 1741. Part of the coast of Chile last seen 93 leagues:

At the break of day discovered the larger of the two islands of Juan Fernandez 11 or 12 leagues … this was a joyful sight to us who were now reduced to an exceeding weakness. At 9 tacked and stood to the eastward …

At length we arrived at the island of Juan Fernandez, in the South Sea, after having several imminent dangers of shipwreck on the coast of Chili… We anchored here on the 16th of June 1741 … just ten days after the departure of a Spanish ship of war which was sent by the Admiral of these seas …

You will be surprised to hear that in a sixty gun ship, on our arrival at this island, we mustered but seventy-two persons, including officers and boys, capable of appearing on deck; the rest being all sick, having lost 228 since our leaving England, which includes nine months.

Meanwhile the *Wager* had been wrecked, and part of her surviving crew mutinied. After the most astonishing adventures the captain and mutineers eventually reached home.

While at Juan Fernandez the *Centurion* was scrubbed, her planking was re-caulked, and the rigging repaired. The squadron now consisted of the *Centurion, Gloucester,* and the *Tryall;* the victuallers had parted company with the squadron according to their contract and the other three ships were presumed lost.

2th June 1741. Juan Fernandez:

Little winds and fair. 2 p.m. HM sloop Tryall anchored here having buried a great number of his men and most of the rest sick …

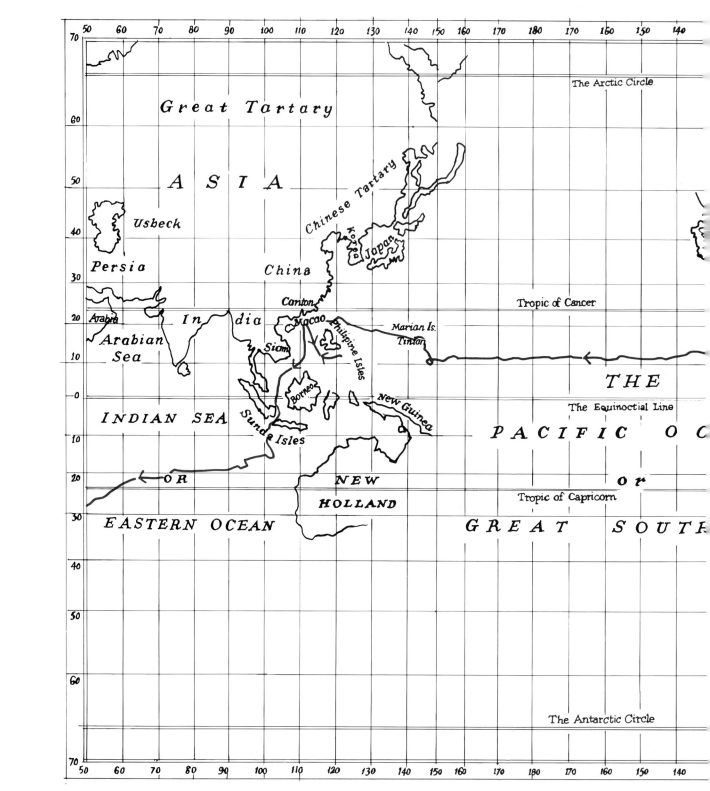

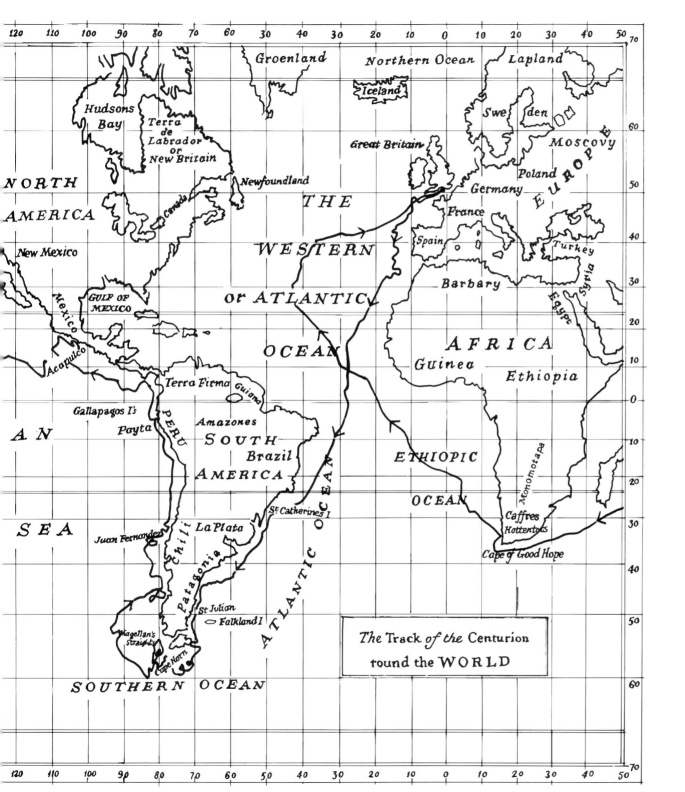

Map showing the known world, published after the circumnavigation.

A View of the COMMODORES TENT at the Island of JUAN FERNANDES.

J. Mason Sculp.

[26]

being employed in sending materials ashore to raise tents for the sick who now died a pace. It being impossible to conceive the stench and filthiness which men lay in or the condition that the ship was in between decks. A.M. got the longboat out. A soldier died.

27th June 1741. Juan Fernandez:

… I went in the boat aboard her [the Gloucester] and found her in a most deplorable condition, nearly two thirds of her men being dead but very few of the rest able to perform their duty.

In first decade of the 18th century, the Scot Alexander Selkirk had been marooned on the island of Juan Fernandez and Daniel Defoe based his story Robinson Crusoe on Selkirk's adventures. Saumarez knew of Selkirk, and commented:- *Their [the goats] flesh was excellent and ate like venison … and perhaps might be the remains of Selkirk's nursery … Their flesh was excellent and ate like venison.*

I shall not attempt a description of this island at present, but only tell you it is the most romantic and pleasant place imaginable, abounding with myrtle trees, and covered with turnips and sorrel. Its bays, teeming with all kinds of fish, seem calculated for the reception of distressed seamen. We stayed here three months, employed in refitting our ships, and restoring the health of the sick …

I cannot omit mentioning the sea lions which seem as extraordinary a production as any in the creation and might justly deserve the observation of an expert naturalists. This surprising creature partakes of a double nature being truly amphibious, and divides its time equally between the land and sea … they bring forth their young which at birth are as big as a seal full grown … When arrived to their full growth they are from 12 to 18 feet long and 9 or 10 in circumference … the males who have a long bulbous substance growing on the top of their head and hangs down three or four inches …

A Sea-Lion and Lioness.

THE BOOTY OF WAR

AT last the English were rewarded with some prizes as the first Spanish merchant ships were captured. General cargo was of little value - they wanted gold and silver.

'The sight of a sail ...'

In the beginning of this month (September) we were agreeably surprised by the sight of a sail to which we immediately gave chase ... We soon after fell in with another, who was her consort, of 500 tons, and much richer, having about 18,000l in money on board, besides a cargo ... Here I commenced captain again, in the Tryal's prize, having twelve guns, besides swivels, with thirty men ...

We next proceeded along to coast of Peru, and took two prizes, both very valuable to the Spaniards, the one being loaded with ship timber, and one other with iron bars, but to us of no great service.

By October 1741 the *Tryall* had become unseaworthy and had to be scuttled.

The Sack of Payta

Anson now decided to attack the town of Payta on the coast of Peru. It consisted of a fort, a garrison, and a few hundred houses with a population of about a thousand - Spanish, mulattos, and black slaves. The shore party, armed with pistols and cutlasses, was commanded by Peircy Brett and Augustus Keppel. As first officer on the *Centurion*, Saumarez remained on board ship.

... we had information of a rich vessel in the road of Paita, bound to Lousuata on the coast of Mexico, the money being still in town. This was a chance worth pursuing: and having arrived off the port in the night, we sent in all the boats manned and armed, with fifty men, surprised and took the town with scarcely any resistance or loss, except one killed and one wounded on our side; the inhabitants abandoning their houses, and retiring to the neighbouring mountains.

The burning of the TOWN of PAYTA on the Coast of
SANTA FEE in the SOUTH SEA.

This event happened on the 15th of November 1741. We kept possession of the town two days and a half without any disturbance from the natives, and, having plundered it, set it on fire, but spared the two churches.

We found here about 30,000l. besides jewels; there was much more, but the inhabitants carried it off. We sunk two galleys and two snows, and carried away with us the small ship that was to have carried the money…

16th November 1741. Island of Lobus SE by S 9 leagues:
Little winds with hot sultry weather. Having plundered and ransacked the town, at 1 p.m. the Commodore gave orders to set it on fire which was immediately executed, several barrels of pitch and tar having been deposited in different places for that purpose; but we spared the two churches … We then steered out to sea leaving the town all in flames.

After taking on water at the island of Quibo the English ships moved slowly up the coast of Mexico in search of the Spanish galleon which sailed every year between Acapulco and Manila laden with treasure. This year they waited in vain.

'A yearly ship whose cargo amounts to an immense sum'

Having watered here [the island of Quibo] *with all imaginable expedition, we sailed hence on the 19th December, with a design to cruise off Acapulco, on the coast of Mexico, for a rich ship that was expected from Manilla, on the island of Luconia, in the East Indies.*

There is a yearly ship whose cargo amounts to an immense sum, and could we but have a favourable passage thither, she must indubitably have been ours; but were disappointed, having been seventy-nine days in effecting a passage which has been performed in twenty, meeting with a long series of calms and uncertain weather. Hence we arrived five weeks too late … We cruized off this port and the coast of Mexico two months, at a distance not to be discovered from the shore …

Having cruised till our water was almost all expended, and having an enemy's coast whereon to replenish, we were obliged to depart ... After many searches, we found a convenient bay for watering called Chequetan, where Sir Francis Drake had refitted. We sunk and burnt all our prizes, in order to cross the great Southern Ocean, and, with the Gloucester in company, go to the East Indies. ...

THE GREAT SOUTHERN OCEAN

AFTER leaving Acapulco the English had to cross the Pacific - then known as the Great Southern Ocean. This was another period of great difficulty and suffering.

We left Acapulco on the 6th of May 1742; and here begins another series of misfortunes and mortality surpassing the first. We had a passage of three months and a half to the Ladrone Islands, which is generally made in two; yet it was a vulgar opinion amongst our people that we had sailed so far as to pass by all the land in the world! Length of time and badness of the weather rendered both our ships leaky; this, joined to our mortality, the scurvy raging amongst us as much as ever ...

The *Gloucester* was in even worse condition than the *Centurion* and had to be abandoned. Now the *Centurion* was alone.

15th August 1742. Acapulco 2126 leagues:

These 24 hours chiefly calm with exceeding hot sultry weather; lay to near the Gloucester under foresail and mizzen. In the evening the Gloucester's long boat came on board with 46 sick men. Most of them very ill. 3 dying in getting over the side ... Mr Dennis Crawley boatsun departed this life, an excellent good officer, with Mr Halldane midshipman and Andrew Slaughter. Our men being very weak and much fatigued but were obliged to look hard to clear the Gloucester.

16th August 1742 Acapulco 22153 leagues:

... our people employed in clearing the Gloucester ... having got as much off as strength and time would permit us the Commander gave orders to set her on fire ... the prospect of the last ship of our squadron blazing within two miles of us combined to make us as melancholy a scene as ever I observed since I have been in the navy.

A View of the Watering Place at TENIAN.

Tinian

We anchored at [an island] *called Tinian, uninhabited, but abounding with wild cattle, hogs, fowls, and fruits: we could not have fallen in with a better place. I am convinced, had we stayed out ten days longer at sea, we should have been obliged to take to our boats, our leak increasing so fast, and our people being all infirm and disabled. We immediately sent all our sick on shore, and began to hope for better times, feeding plentifully on roast beef ...*

29th August 1742. Anchored at the Island of Tinian:

... Thomas Brunnel, armourer, Peter Bell, a boy, John Silks a marine, Abraham MacCarthy, William Angel and Thomas Marshall seamen died.

Macao

After a gruelling passage the *Centurion* arrived at the Portuguese colony of Macao - the only foreign colony on Chinese soil.

By now the *Centurion* was hardly seaworthy and required a complete refit. Anson had to deal with the tortuous Chinese bureaucracy to obtain the stores and labour to carry out the repairs and revictual the ship. It was a long and frustrating stay.

The Chinese were deeply suspicious. They were familiar with Portuguese, Dutch, and English merchants of the East India Companies, but had never before dealt with a British man-of-war.

At long last the Englishmen got permission to proceed with repairs. They had to pay over the odds, but they could afford to do so as they had already got a considerable amount of captured booty.

20th January 1743. Moored a Taipa Quebrado:

Fresh gales and hazy. Sent ashore our booms and spars and cleared our decks of all our lumber. Sent our pinnace and cutter to be hauled up ashore which were much out of repair. 48 caulkers employed on board but a far greater number were expected soon. Agreed to give them 2,000 dollars for careening and completing the ship entirely; this was esteemed a very extravagant price in these parts where day labour is extremely cheap but there was no remedy ...

3th April 1743. Moored at Taipa Quebrado:

Hard squalls with much thunder. Later grew more moderate. Employed in making up our booms, clearing the decks and rendering the ship fit for sea ... Two Mandarin's boats anchored here from Macao being very urgent with us to go away and refusing to assist us with any more necessaries or refreshments, forbidding all the Chinese from coming on board or even selling us anything in the market. The coolies and carpenters were ordered away from us on this occasion.

CAPTURE OF THE COBADONGA

OFFICIALLY the *Centurion* was bound for Batavia and England around the Cape of Good Hope, but Anson's secret plan was to cruise off Cape Espíritu Santo in the Philippines to lie in wait for the Spanish treasure ship - the Manila galleon.

The men practised gunnery and the sailors who were to man the top yards when the galleon was sighted did target practice with their small arms.

20th May 1743. Tobago Xima 201 leagues:
This Cape we proposed to cruise off ... The galleons as we are informed always making this land in their passage from Acapulco ... their usual time of arriving being generally about the middle of June.

At last, on 20th June 1743, the treasure ship was sighted.

The Spanish galleon, the *Cobadonga,* was less heavily armed than the Centurion; it had 44 guns on board, but of these eight were in the hold and only 32 were ready for action. The Spanish had depended on their superior numbers of men (550 compared to the 200 on the *Centurion*).

20th June 1743. Cape Espíritu Santo 8-9 leagues:
At sunrise we were agreeably surprised with the sight of a sail from the masthead in the south eastern quarter, her top gallant sails appearing half out of the horizon. We naturally concluded it must be one of the galleons ... At 11 had her hull entirely out of the horizon ... at μ past noon we took in the topgallant sails and hauled the mainsail up, and soon after hoisted the broad pendant and colours and fired such of the chase and bow guns from alow and aloft as could be brought to bear on her ...

The galleon immediately returned our fire ... His shot were not ill directed, and generally shattered our rigging ...

A view of CAPE ESPIRITU SANTO, on SAMAL, one of the Phillipine Islands, in the latitude of 12:40 N? Bearing WSW distant 6 leagues. In the pos...
presented his Majestys Ship the CENTURION engag'd and took the Spanish Galeon call'd NOSTRA SEIGNIORA DE CABADONGA, from ACAPULCO bound...

Being come abreast of him within pistol shot, the engagement began on both sides with great briskness. Our guns during the whole time being loaded with ball and grapeshot made great havoc, as likewise our tops which were full of our best marksmen …

Our first broadside had a good effect both with his men and rigging. … The enemy on his side kept plying us with his guns and pedros, the latter being loaded with bags of stones, iron nails and musket ball. …

After near an hour's space we observed their fire to abate considerably, and being within three boat lengths of each other could observe the officers running about confusedly as if they were preventing the desertion of their men from their quarters …

After near two hours engagement from our first gun he struck his standard … we hoisted the cutter out, the Commodore sending me on board to take possession of her …

Saumarez was put in command of the captured *Cobadonga*, which was now renamed *Centurion Prize*.

'About a million and a half dollars …'

At my arrival on board I found them in that state of mind the conquered may generally be supposed to be in, being doubtful of the treatment they were to receive, and at the same time had no great opinion of our humanity from the different persuasions in religion, having represented us to themselves as a set of cannibals …

Their decks afforded such a scene as may be supposed after a sharp dispute, being promiscuously covered with carcasses, entrails and dismembered limbs. The main hatchway contained likewise several of their dead which had been thrown down during the action …

The ship was called Nuestra Senora de Cobadonga, commanded by Don Geronimo de Montero, a native of Portugal, which in this service they term General. They had been 12 days from the island of Guam where they watered and refreshed and 72 from Acapulco, at which place they had sold their cargo from Manila, the returns of which amounted to about a million and a half dollars which they had on board, besides private money.

… the ship was surprisingly shattered in her hull, masts and rigging; the mainmast was half shot through, and few of the shrouds left standing … As to our ship, we received several shot on her hull, The foremast and bowsprit had likewise each a shot from the great guns, … In the action one man was killed at his quarters, another died within an hour of his wounds; and a third after an amputation of his leg; and the 2nd Lieut. with fifteen men besides were wounded. Thus ended engagement, in which if the number of our guns and the weight of our metal be impartially considered, it must be confessed we engaged the enemy with great advantages on our side though on the other it may be

objected that they were far superior to us in numbers …

As post-captain of the newly-commissioned King's ship, Saumarez's first task was to transfer the prisoners and the treasure to the *Centurion.*

The Spanish had lost more than 50 dead and 170 wounded. Their General had been wounded by a musket ball in the chest and for several days could not be removed to the *Centurion.*

22nd June 1743. Cape Espíritu Santo 13 leagues, aboard the Centurion Prize:

The weather proved uncertain being subject to squalls and showers of rain. Were employed in sending away the money which besides what was in the passengers' and officers' chests was chiefly contained in small chests containing each 3,000 and others 4,000 dollars …

As the days passed more and more treasure was found aboard the *Cobadonga* hidden in false ceilings and behind panels, some even concealed in a load of cheeses.

26th June 1743. Cape Espíritu Santo 74 leagues:

The 24 hours moderate and fair. Employed in sending the money away; at 6 p.m. sent a launch away loaded, having to the value of 55,000 pounds sterling on board her in chests of silver. Continuing our course to the north west quarter; a.m. swayed the fore topmast up and set the foretopsail; employed in searching the hold … From our first beginning to ship off to this instant esteem by a general calculation that I have sent on board 1,300,000 dollars, besides some wrought plate. Two of our prisoners died of their wounds.

The Spanish prisoners had a miserable time on the *Centurion,* being confined below decks in terrible heat; but they received much better treatment from the English than they had feared. The captain of the *Cobadonga* later wrote to Saumarez thanking the Guernseyman for his kindness and civility.

Both ships were in urgent need of repair and there was no alternative but to return to Macao and the shelter of the Canton River before the storms began which preceded the monsoon season. The Chinese were even less pleased to see the *Centurion* than on the previous visit, but, eventually, the English were able to repair their ship.

It was not until December 1743 that the *Centurion* was able to set sail for home. The prisoners were released with the exception of twenty unmarried men who remained to reinforce the *Centurion's* crew. The *Cobadonga* was sold to Portuguese merchants.

'Bound for England …'

15th December 1743. Anchored Macao Road:

… About noon Mr Nutt, 3rd Lieutenant of the Centurion came on board with the above mentioned Portuguese and certified that the ship was to be delivered up to them. Accordingly, having taken away the colours I embarked with my officers and people and quitting the ship repaired on board the Centurion who weighed anchor and was laying to waiting for our arrival, bound for England.

With no prize ship to command, back on the *Centurion* Saumarez was a 'supernumerary' and his log ceases.

The voyage home, around the Cape of Good Hope, was uneventful. After six months they were back in the English Channel. On 15th June 1744 *Centurion* was anchored at St Helens, Isle of Wight, where the voyage had begun three years and nine months before.

News of the capture of the treasure galleon had preceded her, and when the *Centurion* arrived at Portsmouth the crew was given a heroic reception.

THE GREATEST TREASURE

The *Cobadonga* was the greatest prize ever captured at sea. It took 32 wagons to transport the chests of treasure from the *Centurion* to the Tower of London for safe keeping. The contemporary cash value was reckoned to be more that £800,000 - perhaps £60 million in present-day money. At that time the annual budget of the Royal Navy was less than £3 million.

The epic story of the circumnavigation and the triumphant return of the *Centurion* aroused the popular imagination. Accounts of the voyage appeared in journals and it was celebrated in ballads.

The Achievement

This was the last of the old-style raiding and plundering expeditions and the beginning of a new British interest in the Pacific. And henceforth the Royal Navy fought more sophisticated battles as part of a different strategy.

Commodore Anson's circumnavigation was an astonishing feat of endurance and financially it was a huge success, but it made little difference to the course of the war.

Anson had captured six Spanish merchantmen off the coasts of Chile and Peru, a further six had been destroyed in Payta harbour and the town had been sacked. Fear and alarm out of all proportion to the size of the squadron had been spread through Spanish settlements in Central and South America.

This was achieved with the loss of the *Tryall, the Wager,* and the *Gloucester*. The cost in human life was greater: of the 1936 men who set out from England in September 1740, only 145 returned on the *Centurion*.

Of the five Spanish men-of-war sent to destroy Anson's squadron, only one returned. Both sides lost about the same number of men.

To face death cheerfully ...'

After a spell at Bath to recuperate from the effects of the voyage, Saumarez was soon back at sea.

In 1746 he was in command of the 60-gun *Nottingham*. In an engagement of Cape Clear, he captured the *Mars,* a French man-of-war with 64 guns. The Lords of the Admiralty complimented him for this act of courage and seamanship.

The following year Captain Saumarez again served under Anson and then joined Admiral Hawke. On 14th October, in an engagement off Cape Finisterre, he was hit by a cannon ball and mortally wounded.

The first paragraph of Philip's will reads:-

I, Philip Saumarez, commander of H.M.S. Nottingham, from a reflection of the uncertainty of human life in general, particularly when engaged in a military profession: in order therefore to face death cheerfully, whenever duty of nature shall call upon me, I hereby dispose of whatever Providence has blessed me with …

FURTHER READING

The edited documents which form Philip Saumarez's account of the circumnavigation were published in Leo Heaps's *Log of the Centurion,* Hart David MacGibbon, 1973.

Lord Anson's classic *Voyage Round the World 1740-4* was published in 1748 and has been reprinted many times. It included most of the illustrations reproduced in this booklet. An abridged edition, edited by S.W.C. Pack, was published by Penguin Books in 1947.

Glyndwr Williams: *Documents Relating to Anson's Voyage Round the World 1740-1744,* Naval Records Society, 1967.

Boyle Somerville: *Commander Anson's Voyages into the South Seas and Around the World,* Heinemann, 1934.

Daniel A. Baugh: *British Naval Administration in the Age of Walpole,* Princeton, 1965.

N.A.M. Rodger: *The Wooden World: an Analysis of the Georgian Navy,* Collins 1986, Fontana 1988.

Philip Saumarez's documents and part of his log survive at Sausmarez Manor, other volumes of his log are in the National Maritime Museum at Greenwich. Lord Anson's surviving papers are in the British Library and the Staffordshire Record Office. There are other relevant documents in the Public Record Office at Kew and in the National Maritime Museum.